TABLE OF CONTENTS

Foreword

This book is an expansion of a book I originally wrote for my kids, Hudson and Haley. After many years of seeking God and trying to understand Holy Spirit and have communion with Him, I decided that I wanted my kids to experience at a younger age the same relationship with Him that I have now in my thirties.

After years of pastoring and also starting The Vertical Church in Yuma, Arizona, I realized that not just young children but many adults have never really experienced Holy Spirit in their life. They walk through life powerless and unable to have true joy, peace, patience, kindness, power, self control and love that only he can give. It is as if we have took him and made him an "it" or a "force" or "our weird cousin that we do not want anyone to know about". Sometimes out of fear of what might happen, or out of just sheer ignorance, we have forsaken and forgotten about this third person of the Trinity who plays such an important role in our lives. I hope that this book will inspire you to want to know, commune, experience, and be filled with all of his power, fruit, gifts, and love! In my earlier book for my kids, I keep it pretty simple. I will try to do the same here, but this will be an expansion of my earlier book.

HOW TO READ THIS BOOK

This is a short book that can be read in one setting. However, I suggest that you read it through once, then go back through it again slowly. I also suggest you read this along with your own daily Bible reading plan. Never substitute man's writings for what God is saying to you through His Word. Finally, I would love for you to pass this on to someone else: maybe a family member, friend, or co-worker who wants to know more about walking in power.

CHAPTER ONE

WHO IS THE HOLY SPIRIT?

As a pastor of a church that reaches people far from God, I sometimes feel like Paul must have felt when he came to the church in Ephesus in Acts 19 and asked them this question:

"....Did you receive the Holy Spirit when you believed?" Acts 19:2

To the person who has been in church all of their lives, this question seems elementary. You might answer, "Of course I did!" But what I have found as a pastor is that we live in a post church culture. This means that for the most part the people in the seats who are coming to church for the first time may have never been to church or may be coming back to church after many years out. This creates a gap in understanding. We cannot just assume that everyone knows about the Holy Spirit. In fact, I would argue that many may respond as these disciples did:

"They answered, 'No, we have not even heard that there is a Holy Spirit'" Acts 19:2b

So with this book, I am not going to assume that you know who the Holy Spirit is. I am not going to assume much. I am going to try to simplify all this spiritual talk into a form that will be helpful for you to walk in power day to day.

Before we talk about the fire and power and presence of the Holy Spirit in your life, we must first understand who the Holy Spirit is. We talk much about God the Father, and God the Son; but, it seems that God the Holy Spirit is often times left out of the picture. But remember that they are all three in one. This is called "The Trinity". Trinity is a hard word to understand. In fact, you may have never even heard of the word. It simply means "three in one". It means that God is three persons: Father, Son, and Holy Spirit, yet all one at the same time.

This is hard to understand. That is why it must be believed by faith. In fact, the beginning of understanding that the Holy Spirit is in you starts with faith. It begins with faith in Jesus, the Son, who came and gave

His life for your sins. The Holy Spirit is equal to Father God and Jesus. They are three in one.

While Jesus was here on earth, He was in a human body. He became flesh and bone just like you and I. He lived, breathed, walked, ate, and even used the bathroom! Father God was in heaven and Holy Spirit was present during all of this as well. In fact, we read in Matthew 3 about the baptism of Jesus and see all three there:

"As soon as Jesus was baptized, he went up out of the water. At that moment heaven was opened, and he saw the Spirit of God descending like a dove and lighting on him. And a voice from heaven said, 'This is my Son, whom I love; with him I am well pleased." Matthew 3:16-17

We see here Jesus- The Son, The Holy Spirit- "like a dove" (notice that he was not a dove, but came down like a dove), and The Father God- speaking in a "voice from heaven". All three in the same place working together as one. Again, hard to comprehend but must be believed by faith- the Trinity- Father, Son, and Holy Spirit all three in one Godhead.

So, Jesus was God in flesh. Then Jesus died. Jesus died for your sins and the sins of the entire world. After His death, He rose from the grave. This act of coming back to life was a miracle and a keeping of a promise that He told His disciples. He then rose up into the air and into heaven promising to come again.

But before He died, and before He went back to heaven, He made another promise. He said that when He left, He would send another who would be in us. This was great news. It would be awesome to have Jesus living right there with us day after day telling us what to do and how to act; but, that is not what He did. Think about it, Jesus in flesh and bone could only be in one place at one time; however, if He went away, He would send the Holy Spirit to be in us.

You see the Holy Spirit is God in us. It is Jesus in us. He promised to His disciples in John 14 this:

25 "All this I have spoken while still with you. 26 But the Advocate, the Holy Spirit, whom the Father will send in my name, will teach you all things and will

remind you of everything I have said to you."

Jesus went away and sent the Holy Spirit to be in us. So the Holy Spirit is a person of what is called the "Godhead". He is God in us. He is spirit. As you grasp this, as a new believer or seasoned, understand the importance of him being in you. If he is in us, then we have the power that comes from him. This is how we can walk in power in our day to day lives. Knowing who the Holy Spirit is, is only the beginning. We can have the knowledge, but we need the experience, the immersion, the baptism, the filling, the presence of the Holy Spirit to really learn to walk in power.

CHAPTER TWO

HOW DO I GET THE HOLY SPIRIT INSIDE ME

Before Jesus went to heaven, He said these words to His disciples:

8 But you will receive power when the Holy Spirit comes on you; and you will be my witnesses in Jerusalem, and in all Judea and Samaria, and to the ends of the earth." Acts 1:8

In these words, Jesus was telling His disciples that there will come a time when they will receive or get the Holy Spirit in their hearts. For them that time came in chapter two of Acts in the Bible. In that chapter, we read that the Holy Spirit came upon the people there in power and they began to speak languages that they had never learned. They spoke these languages and the people that heard them were from all over the world and they heard about Jesus in their own language or tongue.

On that day, Peter stood up and preached about Jesus. He said that what these people are experiencing can be yours as well. It is because Jesus lived, died, and then rose from the grave. All they have to do is to repent and be baptized.

Repent means to "turn away". What Peter was saying that day was that they needed to turn away from living for themselves and trying to be good on their own and turn to Jesus for salvation. This is what being "saved", born again, or becoming a Christ Follower or Christian is allb about. It is not about you earning your way into heaven. It is not about you being good enough to pay for your own sins. It is about you coming to a place in your life where you realize that you are a sinner in need of a Savior. Then you must believe God sent Jesus to die for your sins as a payment that you could not pay. As you do that, you are turning away from your self and turning to Jesus for your salvation. This means that you are committing the rest of your life to him. When this happens, there is a great exchange that takes place. You exchange your unrighteousness for the righteousness of God. Now, as God looks at you, He sees the righteousness of Jesus all over you and not your sin. You are forgiven.

The Bible says that on that day 3,000 people gave their lives to Jesus. Peter said in that same chapter that not only will you be forgiven of your sins, but you will receive the gift of the Holy Spirit. In other words, as you believe and are baptized the Holy Spirit will come into your life to live and guide you and teach you in all things.

This means that when you ask Jesus to come into your life and you are baptized by water, the Holy Spirit comes upon you. At the moment of salvation, Jesus moves into your heart as the Holy Spirit. Picture this: The Holy Spirit draws you into that relationship by showing you that you are a sinner and need Jesus. So in essence, as you repent and believe, the Holy Spirit baptizes you into Jesus. Then you are water baptized and all the while Jesus baptizes you into the Holy Spirit. There is a great immersion that happens as now the Holy Spirit is in you. Amazing!!

Now you have the same POWER that Jesus promised in Acts 1:8. You have been given great power and strength because the

Holy Spirit lives in you at the moment of salvation. But keep reading, because the sad part about this is that most Christians do not realize this and never tap into the person inside of them who is the Holy Spirit. Then they never live out their full potential in Jesus. You see, you have been called by God to turn the world upside down. That's right. You! But you cannot do this on your own. You cannot turn the world upside down for Jesus on your own strength. You need a greater power. That power is the person of Holy Spirit who lives in you.

CHAPTER THREE

HOW DO I TAP INTO THE POWER FROM THE PERSON OF HOLY SPIRIT?

Paul, the Apostle, in the New Testament in the book of Ephesians said that we are to be "...filled with the Holy Spirit..." This is an ongoing filling. Not just a one-time event that happens in your life. Everyday of your life is an opportunity for you to be filled and filled again and walk in fullness in the power and presence of Holy Spirit. But how do you do that?

1. Trust in the forgiveness of Jesus continually.

2. Tap into the power of Holy Spirit by asking Him to fill you.

3. Learn to walk in the Spiritual Gifts He has given you.

This 3 step plan is an ongoing process that continues until you are dead and your soul is physically with God. As we live in this world, Jesus is continually working on us and making

us more and more like him. So let's look at
these three steps in detail.

TRUSTING IN THE
FORGIVENESS OF JESUS

When you invited Jesus into your
heart, He forgave you of all your sins. This
means all the sins that you committed in your
past. This also means that Jesus forgave all
the sins that you committed today. At the
same time, Jesus forgave you of all the sins
you will commit in the future.

What this means is that the bad
things that you did yesterday are forgiven, the
bad things you have done today are forgiven,
and the bad things that you may do tomorrow
are forgiven. This is great news. But, it does
not mean that we should live life and do
whatever we want and not worry about
breaking the heart of God.

Understanding that Jesus has forgiven
you should cause you to want to live for Him
and do what He says. This is grace. Jesus has

showed us grace and because of this grace, we should be spurred on to greater works. This helps you know that you are not perfect; but, you are trusting in the perfection of Jesus. So live in a way knowing that God does not condemn or hate you because you may make mistakes, but that God love you and has already forgiven you because of your commitment to Jesus and what Jesus has already done for you on the cross.

You have to basically preach this to yourself daily. I see people all the time, repent and believe in Jesus, get baptized; but, at the first sign of failure or discouragement they give up on God. In reality, they forget that God has already forgiven them. This causes them to continue in sin. If you want to break a sin pattern, then you must come to a place in your life where you realize that you are the righteousness of God in Christ Jesus. You are not the sum of your failures. The anger of God against you has already been satisfied by the cross of Jesus. The brutal and grotesque death of Jesus is a picture of the payment to satisfy the wrath or anger that God has against the rebellion called sin. That was all satisfied for you on the cross. By your repentance and belief, you are adopted into the family of God and no longer have to pay for your sins.

"WOW! Does this mean I can do what I want and there will be no consequences?" If your asking that question, then you might want to ask yourself and ask God to re-shape your heart toward what grace really means. Ask Him to truly do a work on you to show you what this means. I truly believe if you get a true work of grace in your heart, then you will still make mistakes, but you will not have the attitude that you have some sort of license to sin. The truth is that there are always consequences for sin. You may not pay for them like Jesus did on the cross. God still sees you as righteous, but make no bones about it, you will face consequences in this life if you continue in habitual sin.

The reason we are talking about this is because God does not want you to trust in your own good works for your salvation or more power from Holy Spirit. The Holy Spirit is in you and His power and partnership are there. But sometimes we continue doing things that are wrong knowing they are wrong and disobeying Jesus. This causes the power and partnership of the Holy Spirit to be hushed or pushed down inside of you and not used in your life. So we must continually trust in the forgiveness of Jesus and at the same time try to walk and be the hands and feet of Jesus in every thing we do. It is not our good works that produce more power. It is the continual trust in Jesus for the forgiveness of our sins. By trusting in our good works and not His forgiveness, we say to God life is all up to us. So do not trust in your good works, but trust in the forgiveness of Jesus while always seeking Him and His best for your life.

TAP INTO THE POWER OF HOLY SPIRIT BY ASKING HIM TO FILL YOU

As Paul in the New Testament commanded us to be filled with Holy Spirit, this tells us that it is an ongoing action that happens daily. You do not lose the Holy Spirit, you just ask Him to fill you completely and to fullness every day. In fact, a great way to start your day is to pray this prayer:

"Father God, I ask in Jesus name that You would fill me with the Holy Spirit's power, person, and partnership today. Holy Spirit, please be my Senior Partner."

If there is one take away from this book, I would say that to pray this prayer everyday will add power in your life. It will change your life forever. Life will take on a new meaning and you will be filled with God's purpose for your life. He wants to talk with you and lead you and fill you with His gifts so that you can glorify Jesus with your life. But you need to ask Him, everyday to show you what needs to change so that you can become more like Jesus. You have to ask Him to fill you everyday. This is the second key to tapping into the power of Holy Spirit.

As you pray this prayer everyday, you must also read from the Bible. The Bible is God's voice to you. It is one way that God speaks to you. Spending time and walking with the Holy Spirit is about spending time in Bible reading and prayer and talking to Him and listening to Him. Do not forget to spend time in the Bible while you pray everyday. As you open God's word everyday, the Holy Spirit will enlighten you to what God is trying to say to you. This may take some time. I know in my own spiritual walk, the more I read the Bible and ask the Holy Spirit to fill me, the more I understand of the Bible and what God is trying to say to me.

LEARN TO WALK IN THE SPIRITUAL GIFTS HE HAS GIVEN YOU

Each person who asks Jesus into their life gets Spiritual Gifts. The Bible speaks of these gifts in I Corinthians 12-14 and in Romans 12:1-8 and in Ephesians 4. The list below comes from all three of these passages. Here are the Spiritual Gifts according to the Bible:

SPIRITUAL GIFTS
LIST

Apostle: This a person who is sent by God to fulfill a mission from God with strong powers to make it happen. A person who starts a new church might be considered to have the "apostle" gift.

Prophet: This is a person who has the ability, given by Holy Spirit, to communicate a message from God as if God is speaking through them.

Evangelist: This is a person who has a strong desire that all people should come to Jesus and they are going to do all they can to lead people to Jesus and have an ability to draw them to Christ.

Pastor: This is another word for "Shepherd". This means that the person feels that they are called to lead, guide, and direct a group of people toward God's plan for their lives.

Teacher: This is a person who has the ability to explain the Word of God in such a way that it helps the listener understand it better.

The five Gifts that were just listed are sometimes called the "Five Fold Ministry" gifts which usually accompany those who are called into ministry to either be a missionary, pastor, church planter, or preacher.

Service: This is an ability and desire to want to serve others. The person with this gift loves to serve other people without getting anything in return.

Exhortation: That's a big word! But it simply means that this gift is one of saying great things and helping people achieve their best in God. It's the ability to motivate other Christians to do what Jesus wants them to do.

Giving: This gift is the ability to be able to give of your time and resources in a huge way because God has given you the ability and desire to do so.

Leadership: This gift is the ability to influence others to follow a plan that you have come up with and lead them toward greater things.

Mercy: This is having the heart to care for others even those that no one else cares for.

Word of Wisdom: This is a message or word from God that He reveals to you that may or may not be shared with others.

Word of Knowledge: This is a message or word from God that He reveals to you that may or may not be shared with others. This is something that you have not learned, God just gives the information to you.

Tongues: A gift given by Holy Spirit to speak another language that you have not previously learned. It can also be a "heavenly language" or "prayer language" that the Holy Spirit gives you to communicate and build yourself up in faith while praying. This gift is not necessarily to be used in a public worship setting. It can cause great confusion.

Interpretation of Tongues: The ability to make the "tongues" message come alive and be interpreted so that all the church can know the message.

Prophecy: The ability to receive a message from God to build up the church and help the people you are speaking to. Most "prophecy" messages does not contain information about the future.

Working of Miracles: The ability to perform supernatural acts of God by Holy Spirit.

Gifts of Healing: The God given ability to release healing in a person's life by the Power of the Holy Spirit.

Ability to Distinguish Between spirits: The ability to know what is from God and what is not from God. The ability to reveal an evil spirit and bring God's power and purpose in it's place by the blood of Jesus.

Faith: Knowing what you hope for, and having a sure understanding of things you do not see.

UNDERSTANDING THE GIFTS

These gifts are not a popularity contest. Just because you have one gift and another person has a different gift or multiple gifts does not mean that you are greater than they are or that they are greater than you. Not everyone has the same gift mix. I believe that the Holy Spirit has all of these gifts and He will manifest any one He needs into your life as you need them. This means that if you desire any of these gifts, you can pray and ask the Holy Spirit to manifest these gifts in you. But also ask Him to show you what your specific gifts are.

Sometimes we get caught up into which gift I may have or do not have. God does not want you to lay awake at night wondering what He has gifted you with. Do not worry about finding these gifts just walk with Holy Spirit knowing that He will give you the ability that you need to carry out God's plan in your life. So do not worry; however, there is great value in seeking out which gifts you might have.

Steps To Finding Your Spiritual Gifts

1. **GET ALONE WITH GOD** This is your opportunity to put into practice what you have been reading. It is one thing to learn about the things of God it is another to actually apply them. So right now, stop reading. Get alone with God and....

2. **ASK HIM TO SHOW YOU YOUR SPIRITUAL GIFTS** Do not be afraid to just come out and ask God to show you what He has gifted you with.

3. **READ OVER THE LIST WITH SPIRITUAL EYES** As you stop, get alone with God and ask Him to show you your gifts, read over the list again. This time, allow the Holy Spirit to let the ones that He is gifting you with to pop out of the page in such away, you know that this is the route he is leading you. Then...

4. **ASK HIM TO FILL YOU AND GIVE YOU THE POWER TO WALK IN THE GIFTS** Take this time and ask Jesus to fill you again with the Holy Spirit's power so that you may operate and walk in power daily through the gifts He has given you.

If there is a special gift you want the Holy Spirit to give you, then pray and ask Him.

So Let's review:

1. The Holy Spirit lives in you as you ask Jesus to come into your life.

2. The Holy Spirit wants to fill us with His power and to walk with Him daily.

3. To tap into The Holy Spirit's person and power we must:

    a. Trust the forgiveness of Jesus continually.

    b. Ask Him to fill us daily.

    c. Learn to walk in the power of our Spiritual Gifts.

What Are My Next Steps?

1. Start reading the Bible every day.

2. Pray every day that Holy Spirit would fill you to fullness.

3. Pray all day long. Just talk to the Holy Spirit as you go through your day.

4. Learn about your gifts and walk in them. Learn from others with the same gifts.

5. Ask the Holy Spirit to fill you with fire!

6. Change the world!!! Turn it upside down!!! God has gifted you and the Holy Spirit is in you!!!!

CONCLUSION

TURN "WHAT IF" INTO "COULD BE"

This may be the end of the book, but it is not the end of the power life that God has called you to. What if every believer in Jesus truly walked daily in the power that the Holy Spirit gives? What if we all took seriously the call to be the hands and feet of Jesus? What if, like the early church, we operated daily as the church in the same power that they had?

Personally, I believe that "what if" actually "could be". I always have. Ever since I was a young teenage kid just finding my bearings with Jesus, I believed that the greatest days of the church are still ahead. As an adult trying to walk in power daily, I still believe that the best is yet to come. There has to come a moment in every believers life where they realize that they are not called to just set in a church Sunday after Sunday and call that "the Christian life". That there is more to it than just sitting and soaking it all in and then going back to our mundane lives. Jesus died for us so that He might live in and

through us for the glory of the Father. He left
and gave us the Holy Spirit to be able to walk
in that abundant life power daily. It is time
you unleash that power and start today
walking in power!

ACKNOWLEDGEMENTS

I want to acknowledge some people that inspire me to write something like this. My wife, Melissa has believed in me from day one. Most of all, she has believed in God's call on my life. She has trusted me as the spiritual leader of our home and has loved me like Jesus does! Secondly, my kids inspired me to write this book. I see in them a potential for greatness that far reaches any book, sermon, or enterprise that I start or am involved with. I want them to have spiritual knowledge and application earlier in life so that they can turn this world upside down. My staff at The Vertical Church is wonderful! They allow me to take time to write, preach, cast vision, study God's Word, and lead this generation to be the hands and feet of Jesus. I want to say a special thank you to Danny Wells, our Executive Pastor, at The Vertical Church who did the artwork for the cover of this book. Danny is one of many who embody the vision of being the hands and feet of Jesus. Last, I want to acknowledge the wonderful body of Christ called The Vertical Church. You spur me on to greater things!

With that said, The Holy Spirit inside of me produces words that are not my own. If you are touched by anything that I say, remember that it is Jesus through the Holy Spirit using my weak vessel. I give all glory, honor, and praise to Him, Jesus- My Senior Pastor, and to the Holy Spirit- My Senior Partner, and to Father God- My Senior Provider- all three in one supply my every need.